Baltimore ORIOLES

KENNY ABDO

Fly!
An Imprint of Abdo Zoom
abdobooks.com

abdobooks.com

Published by Abdo Zoom, a division of ABDO, P.O. Box 398166, Minneapolis, Minnesota 55439.

Printed in the United States of America, North Mankato, Minnesota.
102025
012026

Photo Credits: Alamy, AP Images, Getty Images, Shutterstock
Production Contributors: Kenny Abdo, Jennie Forsberg, Grace Hansen
Design Contributors: Candice Keimig, Neil Klinepier

Library of Congress Control Number: 2025936766

Publisher's Cataloging-in-Publication Data

Names: Abdo, Kenny, author.
Title: Baltimore Orioles / by Kenny Abdo
Description: Minneapolis, Minnesota : Abdo Zoom, 2026 | Series: MLB teams | Includes online resources and index.
Identifiers: ISBN 9798384940111 (lib. bdg.) | ISBN 9798384940876 (ebook) | ISBN 9798384941255 (read-to-me ebook)
Subjects: LCSH: Baltimore Orioles (Baseball team)--Juvenile literature. | Baseball teams--Juvenile literature. | Professional sports--Juvenile literature. | Sports franchises--Juvenile literature. | Major League Baseball (Organization)--Juvenile literature.
Classification: DDC 796.357--dc23

Table of CONTENTS

ORIOLES

The Baltimore Orioles have built a nest of great players and unforgettable moments. Each game offers the team a chance to spread its wings and soar to new heights in baseball!

Baltimore
25

The Orioles continue gliding through ups and downs while keeping fans' spirits soaring!

Orioles
31
Orioles

BATTER UP!

The Orioles began play in 1901 as the Brewers in Milwaukee, Wisconsin, but lasted just one year. They spent 50 years in St. Louis, Missouri, as the Browns. In 1954, the team moved to Baltimore with the nickname the Orioles, after Maryland's state bird.

WINGARD
WILLIAMS
DURST
DAVIS
GERBER
LAMOTTE
ST. LOUIS
AMERICAN
JONNARD
C. ROBERTSON
HARGRAVE
E. ROBERTSON
AUSTIN
GIARD
CONLON PHOTOS

Orioles
5
8

In 1966, the Orioles won their first World Series by **sweeping** the Dodgers 4–0. Star players like Frank Robinson and Jim Palmer helped lead the way. The victory marked the start of a golden **era** for the team.

Third Base
Brooks Robinson
BALTIMORE
ORIOLES

The Orioles were back on top in 1970 with another World Series win! After defeating the Reds, Brooks Robinson was named MVP. He recorded sixteen putouts and eight assists, locking down the Reds' powerful lineup.

GRAND SLAMS

In 1983, the Orioles won their third World Series. With Eddie Murray and Cal Ripken Jr. leading the way, the Orioles defeated the Phillies. It remains one of the team's greatest moments.

The Orioles had a rough start to the 1988 season, losing their first 21 games. By 1989, the Birds bounced back and finished second in the **American League** (**AL**) East.

Camden Yards opened its doors in 1992. That year, more than 3.5 million fans flocked to the ballpark! It was one of the highest attendances in Major League Baseball history.

RIPKE
8

Cal Ripken Jr. became a baseball legend in 1995 when he broke Lou Gehrig's **record** for most games played in a row. His streak of 2,632 games played helped earn him the nickname "Iron Man," showing his strength and love for the game.

Orioles

Under **manager** Buck Showalter, the Orioles returned to the **postseason** in 2012 and 2016. In 2012, the Orioles moved on to the **AL Division** Series, but lost to the Yankees. By the end of the decade, the team faced struggles that led to a major shake-up for future success.

In 2023, the Orioles rocked a 101–61 **record**. They won the **AL** East title for the first time since 2014 and celebrated their first season with more than 100 wins since 1980.

The team finished the 2024 season in second place in the **division** with a **record** of 91–71. Fans hoped the Orioles would keep that momentum in seasons to come.

HALL OF FAME

Frank Robinson won the **Triple Crown**, was named the **AL** MVP, and led the Orioles to their first World Series win all in 1966. Over his career, Robinson went to 14 **All-Star Games**, earned All-Star Game MVP honors, and more! Robinson was named to the Baseball Hall of Fame in 1982.

F. ROBINSON
20

Cal Ripken Jr. was famous for his strength and reliability. He recorded 3,184 hits and set a **record** with 2,632 back-to-back games played. In 1983, Ripken led the Orioles to clinch the World Series title. He was **inducted** into the Baseball Hall of Fame in 2007.

Orioles
8

Cedric Mullins was a key player for the Orioles from 2018 to 2025. Known for his power and speed, he was selected for the 2021 **All-Star Game**! That same year, Mullins became the first player in Orioles history to join the **30–30 club**.

STRAUSS
MAX
MULLINS
WILDCARD

GLOSSARY

30-30 club – a group of batters who have collected 30 home runs and 30 stolen bases in a single season.

All-Star Game – a yearly baseball contest where top players from the AL and the National League (NL) compete against each other.

American League (AL) – one of two 15-team leagues that make up MLB.

division – a number of teams grouped together in a sport for competitive purposes.

era – a period of time in history.

inducted – brought in as a member.

manager – or field manager, the equivalent of a head coach who is responsible for overseeing and making final decisions.

postseason – the playoffs, including the wild-card round, divisional playoffs, league championship series, and World Series.

record – a team's season total of wins and losses; also a top achievement by a player or team that no one has done before.

sweeping – winning all games in a series.

Triple Crown – an achievement earned when leading the league in batting average, home runs, and runs batted in (RBIs) in the same season.

ONLINE RESOURCES

To learn more about the Baltimore Orioles, please visit **abdobooklinks.com** or scan this QR code. These links are routinely monitored and updated to provide the most current information available.

INDEX